unbridled

by

Jacqueline Oby-Ikocha

Moyhill Publishing

ISBN 9781905597772

A CIP catalogue record for this book is available
from the British Library.

Designed & typeset by Moyhill Publishing.

Printed in USA.

Dedication

For love

and those

who keep me sane

Contents

Contents

Contents

Scattered rain

My heart pours out,
my soul follows;
in drip drops of words
into buckets of pages
like a pail set under the eaves of rusty zinc
to gather drops of scattered rain.

Bleeding Heart

I bleed,
in ways that
your eyes can never
see

shattered heart
I tie up
with multiple strings.

Hush!

Hush! Let's keep silent.
Speak not of these things;
if we pretend hard enough
they'll certainly go away.

Hush! Silence is solemn.
We swallowed our naked truth
not to blind your reality;
we're buried in composts of misery.

Hush! We kept silent.
Dancing quietly with monsters
hidden under our beds
until they became us.

Us

There are us.
Born at the edge of a void
where there is no beginning
early memories blurred
by recollections of bouncing on uncle's laps
where turgid erections caressed our baby butts.

There are us.
Sitting alone all night
erasing ourselves and playing cracked records
from torturous nightmares of useless rape
forcefully fucked and threatened with grim death
where safety is far and we can't seem to get away.

There are us.
Who have felt emptied
by those who take want they want
leaving us feeling less than whole
plotting their demise in inconceivable ways
where we pray for peace to find us.

In My chamber

You are welcome into my inner chamber
but, do mind your head!
For I am tossing huge rocks
at the demons that besiege me
and taunt at my door

You could come into my inner chamber
but, you'll do well to mind your feet!
For I am breaking glass
and there are shards of broken glass
that would pierce your dainty feet

You could come into my inner chamber
but, keep your ears plugged!
For I am screeching at ear-splitting decibels
and spewing a torrent of words
that might leave you perplexed and overwrought

You know what, it's a bad idea,
you should stay out there!
'Cos it's probably safer outside.
Don't come into my inner chamber
lest you get caught in the sizzling fray.

For Sale

Your ancient thigh is full of worlds
yet you've not lived for so long.
Only eight, they say you are
but painted as a doll
your eyes look older than life.

Your narrow chest with tiny nubs
have felt more manly hands than you can count
you are told that this is the way it is.
That between your thighs lies a drive thru
for men who pay to stop by.

Your skin grows numb from dirty demands
and frequent visits to your cage of plight.
The fire in your bright eyes slowly dies
violence seeps and corrodes your blood,
broken, your dreams buried before they were born.

Born Black

When I was born I had two strikes on me
being born female and being born black.
Dark pigment of my skin decides where I belong;
a second-class citizen at the bottom of the human
    barrel,
the sex between my legs carries her own baggage;
it didn't matter if I loved trucks I got the painted
    blue-eyed dolls.

When I was born I came with all my dreams
I didn't know that society had its dreams for me.
Providing labels to confine you in neat boxes
enclosing you where they want you to be.
I refuse to be labelled, described like goods for
    supermarket shelves,
who I am, is my business to learn for myself.

When my voice is strong, I am called aggressive,
the typical angry black woman
lest my voice goes soft, I am weak, unsure and you
    are suspicious;
that I don't quite fit your stereotyped box.
To be a woman can be exhausting for sure;
a black woman, now that's a double score

My journey growing up as a black woman
has taught me a lot about the world,
that I must work twice as hard to claw out of a box,
to try even harder to be heard without prejudice
and with the burden placed on my shoulders
to walk tall, live without apologies and to never be
    ashamed of being me.

Let me tell you, it's amazing to embrace my rich
    culture,
intricately woven by the tapestry of time,
to be black is an identity I wear with pride.
Melanated skin glowing smooth with life
springy, textured hair adorned in different styles,
resilience is stored within my bloodied veins.

I have come to realize through lifes' lessons,
that in truth when all is said and done,
colour, sex and your labels don't count,
what I make of my life is what matters most.
It's not my business to keep you comfortable and
    in control by staying confined in your box,
'cos when I was born, I came alone and when I go, I
    go alone.

Illusive

I am overfed from chewing the fat on Proverbs 31
 woman
an elusive yardstick used to measure my virtue,
 nobleness and beauty,
whilst your low bars of expectation and braying is
 accepted as acceptable
and ugly misogyny gets waved away as manliness

In the face of your chauvinistic mannerisms
playing dumb and docile has never been my forte,
asking me to submit to silence and
to hold my opinion gets you the drop-dead
 side-eye.

'Don't you know that I am made noble,
that beauty is not bequeathed by you,
that my flame may burn slow, yet my embers are
 fiery to touch;
that I'm a shapeshifter resilient beyond your
 words?'

I have sat at the spindle from dusk to dawn,
weaving finery for you to seat at the city gates,
but know that my illusive calm comes with
 complex wisdom
that your simple mind can never begin to fathom.

I See Colours

Life would be insipid without differences between
    you and I,
from gorgeous ebony to alabaster skin and all the
    hues in between,
I see a world of beautiful people.

When you say *'you don't see colours'*
I trip in a haste to apologize
for the poor state of your sight;

then I notice that your colour selection
or lack thereof, applies to others different from you,
and not to the beauty of nature's reflections.

You are well able to tell beautiful red roses,
from orchids, tulips, bougainvilleas and grass,
spots on the Tiger you see well in 3D poses;

you oh and ah over a puppy's breath,
at willowy wisps of cloud you sigh in wonder,
but fellow humans you treat with stealth.

Don't offer me those political condescending words,
or your porous thoughts of inclusion, do please
    spare me;
the Earth belongs to all, don't be absurd!

I do apologize for your loss of appreciation,
for lack of depth to see the beauty of humanity
   around you,
that I believe, must be a dreary and tiresome
   introspection.

I Am Judging You

'Why do you write like this,
don't you worry that people will sit and judge?'
she asked me.
'I've grown too old to worry about being judged;
for judgement has been my portion for as long as I
    know,'
I replied.
I don't shield my words in niceties,
afraid to cause you to blush.
I don't say my words to cause shame,
but yes, I'm judging you.
I can't pretend that we are friends enough
to write things only relatable
and swallow my words to please you
'cos that would be dishonest,
I'll be lying to myself.

Cracked Prisms

Lost in the wilderness of her heart
she looked at the cracked prisms of her life,
shattered dreams, broken marriage, lost livelihood;
bare tattered ribbons of hope
of who she knew she was.
She held fast,
afraid to disappear
and no one would notice.
Biting pangs of hunger
and pain that coursed through her mind
reminded her that she's alive and
like the oak that knew itself
even when it was an acorn,
she had to survive.

Walks Far

barefoot, on the lonely path
she made her way out
dragging along
a bag of guilt
and resignation
that bent
her
bones

she has walked far
yet never far enough
serving time
for his life
still took
toll on
her
life

many times, she wished
she could change
the hands of time
and the blows
that life
had
dealt
her

if only she had
walked far away
when he first
started the
slaps that
grew to
bashing
her

the nightmare would
have been cut short
and the
kitchen knife
would have
never been
used.

Beaten

He never laid hands on her
yet he battered her,
with brooding forbidden silence
he broke her.
Emotional rag doll
adapted to swinging moods,
tiptoeing on eggshells
not to break fragile ego.

The days were long and hard
smiles are worn and gone
the silence of the nights ominous
dark handsomeness turned savage,
ensnared in a sticky web
sleek tongue tossed daggers and
fiery eyes' shot bullets.

Nagging

Your lips are smooth as silk
and burn like the blacksmiths rod,
your words eat away at my flesh
they crack the roof of my brain,
your constant tapping like a woodpecker
exhausts me into my mental shell.

Hangman's Noose

Purple bruises encircled her neck,
her skin the canvas for punches and slaps,
silky long hair the hangman's noose
entwined in a cord he easily grabs.

Nerves whittled to a sorry mess,
nails bitten down to a stumpy nub,
discoloured patches covered with dresses,
a wretched attempt to cover up her stresses.

How long she sat in bewildered tears,
patching bruises and dreaming getaways,
the handgun waved at her head was a nightmare,
next weeks' news he was blown away.

Stir it Up

Buttercups, cover up!
Don't show that bit of neckline, or let it plunge to a
cleavage, you don't want to stir it up.
You mustn't flash that tell-tale ankle or the
appendages of your legs except you want to stir
it up.

Buttercups, what of your seductive hair?
Keep it tight in a bun and hurry to safety before the
sign of dusk except you want to stir it up.
You are risking it when you dress like a skank, for
sure you deserve to be spanked, you must have
stirred it up.

Buttercups my girl, I dare to ask; where are your
sexual rights?
Pieces of your body always objectified, yet you are
constantly denied.
Your breasts are great for sucking, your mouth
designed for blowing, your face good for
showing, your pussy to be grabbed for fucking.

Buttercups, don't dare protest your pride!
You are only to be seen, Heaven forbid, but not to
be heard. Except to express squeals of pleasure
and stoke his ego with endless adulations.
Behind a dumpster, she was violated and trashed,
vilified, she deserved it, how dare she go out?

Buttercups, who do you call?
No one wants to hear. The cops are the boys, the
    judge is out of town. They all say, Oh! The boys
    are just being boys.
Your do's and don'ts grow by milliseconds, yet
    there are hardly any for the boys. Let's excuse
    them, they are simply sowing wild oats.

Buttercups, you stirred it up.
You know you did and we all know what that
    means. Oh, what predators they've become.
    Their wild rage for sexual gratification unable to
    be contained, it must be your fault.

Maybe you spoke too little or too much, you
    danced a lot, you laughed out loud, you walked
    alone, you jogged alone, you flashed your ankle,
    you looked him in the eyes, you rode the bus,
    you went to the library, to the grocery, to cinema
    or the mall, maybe it's none of the above, but it
    must be your fault, you stirred it up.

Buttercups my girl, where is your voice?
You are groped, poked, harassed and bludgeoned;
    yet you get to bear the stigma and hang your
    head in shame.
Maybe when you find your rights your burden will
    be light.

Gatecrashers

Uninvited, they arrive.
I smell them from miles away
their radar zeros into the crowd
they steal in to join the happy gang.

Their presence disturbs and stifles,
like thieves they are up to no good
planting themselves on both sides like guards
the silent battle of my mind starts.

My other self, the invisible one
vacates in a hurry to watch from the other side,
'Do they know your secrets?' depression asks in its
    know-it-all voice,
*'I bet you wouldn't be the belle of the ball if they
    knew,'* loneliness opines.

Lips crack a smile, false laughter rings in the room,
intelligent conversation over glasses of wine,
breezy kisses blown into the air of cheek sides,
troubles forgotten maybe till tomorrow or less.

We do know how to throw great parties, our
    mannequin faces caked in powder,
I count minutes before it's alright to escape,
with depression and loneliness dogging each step
    I take,
making such ruckus as we jostle out of the room.

Silence Screams

Shrill silent scream persists in my throat
a wild fox of rampaging moods
eager to jump out to yip and howl
angst, vapid thoughts, melancholy, ticking
    nerves...

A riot of quivery emotions,
an interwoven lattice of racing ruminations,
gridlocked, constriction grows to combustions
    levels,
anxiety waits outside the door...

Bright painted inexpressible thoughts pressure the
    mind,
edgy fluttering nervousness attacks the bowels,
silence screams on the sidewalk and corners,
shivering like a tired leaf tossed around in the
    storm.

Mumbled Mutterings

Unbidden, hidden memories of the past
scratch the surface of my mind
with desperate intensity
begging to be let out.

Fevered Fascination

Engraved, these cloying memories
become images of torment
like little imps sitting on my chest
to dog my night in insomnia.

Fighting Fierce

Breathless, ensuing battle
of timeless nightmare rises,
determined to erase such senseless struggle
I cut off my hand.

For Salome

You were beaten down
but you refused to rest fallen,

He burst your brains
but your grey matter wouldn't spill,

Stepped all over you
prickles of your pride punctured his feet,

He chewed you up to swallow
but you held his throat and he nearly choked,

He pummelled you with all his might
his arms became useless tools,

Bruised and left in the grounds to die
you held on with all your life,

With fierce pride in your blackened eye's
and a crooked smile on broken lips,

Determination in your aching bones,
you crawled out of the crack to light.

Exchange

She sold them
one by one.
The valuable pieces
traded in the shadows of pain
for mere offerings of peace.
Her dreams she left
at the altar bereft,
her voice she sold
for the silence of gold,
her pride she traded
it was too complicated,
emptied of everything
she became nothing.

Let it Go

The more I lingered
hoping to patch it up
the more we got torn apart
it was better to let it go

It was not
that I didn't believe in us
but I loved us too much
it was slowly killing me

The Breakup

When she found secret love
in the arms of another,
he called her promiscuous
and branded her a two-bit slut.

He forgot his days of dodgy pass,
the numerous trips out of town
and philandering pastimes,
of course, they didn't count.

He forgot the belittling and the neglect,
the slave ship of harsh, abusive words,
the plague of lies, deceit and malcontent
of course, they didn't count.

In acrimony, he took the dog,
and she got the two cats.
Everything else he split into half,
he made sure he did it with an axe.

Nine Yards

I gave you nine yards
you took ten
I gave till,
there was nothing left to give.

Forgiveness is not only for you
I need to forgive myself too,
for giving you everything
till
I had nothing to give myself.

Stolen Desire

Deep moans she breaths into his mouth,
limbs curved around his taut body in an age-old
    dance,
careless whispers he utters in her ears,
a necklace of passion planted around her neck,
faster and faster pleasure takes her apart.

Eyes wide awake, she's all alone,
the door is locked, his side of the bed cold,
musky scent hung in the air, a testament to his lost
    presence,
like a fickle weather, that never stays
he goes back and continues to live a lie.

Wrong

I didn't like it
but I let you do it
I wanted to be special
so, you would like me

I was wrong
not special to you at all
there were too many of us
who let you do it

Bitter Truth

Sorrow met her
at the doorstep
where her heart
dared fall in love

through misty eyes
she watched them,
their passionate embrace
blatantly said it all

Running Man

Daddy is not a word you inherit
by planting active sperm cells
down those vagina walls.

Like a rolling stone, you rumble along
dangling all the misses to your bedchamber
your prowess proven, many bairns you left forlorn.

Like a wimp, you have all the excuses,
never living up to your responsibilities
except letting down your breeches and calling
    them bitches.

Like a boy, you run from manly duties,
afraid that if you stopped running
old age would certainly catch up with you.

But age sure does a faithful number
that no running or surgeon's knife can change,
and when you are worn out, you'll certainly be
    estranged.

Stalking

Priceless parts of me I gifted you,
fingered, squeezed, sucked to your delight
you shove them aside like castaway toys,
they no longer interest you.

I sit. Redundant. A broken doll.
Misused, abandoned, unloved, lost,
left in the mouldy attic,
gathering cobwebs and dust.

I watch you. Attempts to block me pitiful.
In throes of passion, you forgot
that I have your passwords
and know how your mind works.

Didn't you know my feelings
when you chose to toy with me?
You call me clingy, weird, stalker,
words thrown at a flimsy whim.

You should have left me
in the plain of dull seasons
than to awaken my heart
flung into vast fields of ruin to die.

Stalking you becomes a pastime
Like a black widow spider
I spin my web in earnest
waiting for you to come.

Sugar Daddy

All she now wanted was a place to feel loved, to
    spread her hair and stretch out lissom limbs, not
    - the luxuries that screamed *'you owe me,'* - kept
    by a lord who assessed each room in suspicion.

All she wanted was someone to hold her, but
    he said, *'your nipples possess sensitive things,'*
    handing bags of goodies from hairy knuckles, a
    slow kiss a token for his prize.

There's hardly anything to say anymore, spreading
    midriff untucked from a shirt one size too small,
    resting receding hairline on silk pillows to watch
    her do racy stuff that got racier by the moment.

'Take off my shoes and come here baby,' in lowered
    timbre like the main daddy, briskly they slip
    into sexual mambo with his animal pants
    ringing through the house accompanying her
    pretentious squeals that made her cringe.

All she wanted was passion that made her mad,
    a lover to love her wild heart recklessly; not to
    listen to his snores of replete satisfaction when
    she was nowhere near satisfied.

All she wanted was to stop staring out of the
    window, sipping Irish cream and puffing perfect
    smoke rings like signals for rescue, while nursing
    curdled lumps of dissatisfaction that growled in
    her blood.

A Moment of Silence

All she wanted was some respite
from taunting eyes.

All she wanted was to be rescued
from bullying voices,

that bit into her flesh like barbed wire
eyes burning her like raging fire.

All she wanted was to get out
of the prison that wearied her,

that enclosed her with dark monsters
who roamed the jungle of her mind.

All she felt was desperation
for a moment of blissful relief

All she got was her moment of silence
that came from the little bottle of pills.

Razor Blade

Living became her struggle
tempting droplets offered succour
clinging to sanity a battle lost

The blade sliced with jagged lines
Sharp razor teeth tearing into veins
Life's precious blood slowly seeped away.

Tatters

Why they call it glad rags I fail to understand
wearing them certainly didn't feel glad to me.
Paper thin, worn state flapping in the winds
tattered, it barely held my bones in place.

Glad! That's not how to describe these rags
that barely kept me from freezing'
the biting fingers of merciless drift
seeped into my frail skin.

Paupers hand-me-down were no longer easy to
    come by,
they barely covered me from uncensored eyes
who looked away quickly when mine met theirs
yet stared in longing secret like dogs after meat.

At Streets Edge

He straddles poverty
a spare meal for the day
satisfies his bones

He sits at the edge of the street
with his dirty plastic plate
and pleading in his eyes

They think he's a druggie or lazy bum
failing to know that he's just a man
who fell hard on hard times

For no man prefers to scrounge
for food in the trash collector
instead of dining in his house.

Underfed

In silence, I sat
waited in futility
hoped in hopelessness
that you would bring me words
that would make a difference.

Breath bated expectantly,
I perspired in speculation
hanging on to miserable offerings
you starved me;
you kept me hungry.

Wearied, I became a deviant
tired of the hollow craving
for words, I desperately needed.
In vain, I no longer waited
my own words I wrote and fed myself.

Missing

In every crowd
he searched,
at every turn
every face resembled hers.

Waiting

Every day, he stood at the misty moors
waiting for her to come,
through the fog he saw her form
the whistling winds carried her voice.

He waited. He waited. He waited in futility;
Till the sun rose to brighten the grey,
melted away, the mist disappeared
along with her floating voice and foggy form.

To the lonely cabin, he returned,
the beef and chilli soup had long grown cold;
a favourite from the recipe she left behind
he ate in silence and mused aloud,
tomorrow, he will be at the moors to wait again.

Stuck

She left that place
but she never got anywhere else,
'cos her heart was stuck
lost right in the place that she had to leave.

My Sins

I have sinned
in ways that you wouldn't understand.
Some I remember,
and some my mind refuses to recall.
Some I am paying for,
and some the bills are yet to come.
Since I am told
that there's nothing new under the sun,
therefore, I can safely assume
that you share some of my sins too.

Hidden Rose

Fearing the truth that her existence betrays they
    buried her to deny her presence.

Hoping she would suffocate without nurture
her wings were clipped to prevent escape.

Bound. Caged in.
She despised the strictures of such control.

Feather by feather in decay,
she bloomed as a scarlet rose in the dark.

Lost and Found

Even as you are caged
you'll keep singing
now that you know
that your lost voice
has been found
for your ears.

Disjointed

My heart stopped beating when it happened,
I think for sure I must have died.

The screeching tires wouldn't stop,
it went on and on and on and on….

in milliseconds, your body slammed into the car in
    a sickening thud,
the most awful sound I'd ever heard.

Somersaulting, I tumbled over and over at a slow
    endless speed,
legs and arms flew in different directions in a
    macabre dance,
petrified screams hung in the air…
whose voice was that horrified screech, it was
    mine, I'm afraid it was.

Blood-shot eyes and broken bones,
I gathered my wounds to withdraw to the morgue,
    where lifeless bodies lined up one by one.

I could smell his life, my life, our lives,
two stories crossed in one scene, one act,

dreams, plans, futures disembowelled, frozen for
    split moments as they gradually dissipated, into
    a void where the free fall never seemed to end.

Life left him at 1:05pm, dealing him a bitter blow;
mine a rhapsody of a disjointed story.

I Saw Death

Bam!
In a blink,
everything changed.

He fought,
grasping to hold on
but he lost

His life
extinguished in a
quiet storm.

Leftovers

Life, we live in miserable scraps.
Leftovers, of everything we choose to keep
hidden in dark crevices of our souls
saved for days that never come.

Of love, we give in sketchy patches,
smiles coaxed unwilling out of us,
good thoughts measured with stinginess
kindness is a foreign word.

Leftovers we have everywhere,
saving them was smart or so we think,
with greed, we grab at all we can get
not caring if the man next door breaks his bread.

We hoarded our gifts like stingy wuss,
they became a landfill for graves covered with moss,
leftovers we kept till the last days of our race,
and then it became too late to embrace.

Empty

That emptiness in you
you've filled with trinkets and toys,
momentarily you bought happiness,
yet sadness shines in parts of you,
where no toys can touch.

In Memory

His anguish is a writhing entity
binding him in a choke hold.
Digging into parts of him
stabbing with fiery intensity
like a fresh wound stung
by thousand soldier ants.

He was losing his mind
wanting to gouge it out
from his splitting heart
to look at it, palpate and taste it,
no comfort did he accept or seek
wrapping his loss like a warm cloak.

In the chilly night of life,
how did life so full of life
and laughter cut short amid laughter?
In minutes, she'll be lowered for closure
but he doubted if his gaping sores
would ever close again.

Don't Cry

He was told not to cry
that it wasn't manly enough,
so, he drowned in his tears
where his bottled sobs
made him a total wreck.

Death

It's given that a man only dies once
laid out with arms folded in front of him
in this pose he journeys back to dust
all his toil now done and gone.

Some break their bodies all through time,
some sit drunk and screw their wives through hell
    and back,
many swallow their worlds and live hating
    themselves,
but when night comes all of us will die.

It's given that a man only dies once,
but some have dreamt their death at the sight of the
    bomb,
some wake from their dream to try to live some more,
and many will die with those dreams in their mind.

Storm

Justice hides her head in shame,
Karma looks on with open eyes,
I come to you with a heart of peace,
but my parts you tear to pieces.

My children you've strung up to hang,
dismembered in cold blood,
their bits spill across your fields,
their souls sigh in lonesome mourn.

Through the wide vista of your eyes,
I see greed, war and mayhem,
your tongue forked, mesmerizing like rattlesnakes,
lies you drink with blood and red wine.

Your ghosts asleep in comfort
in big houses on the green and brown hills,
and mine roams the open prairies
listening to the coming storm.

The Nightmare

In these days of our lives
I have seen the birth of the nightmare.
The shield is replaced by the spear,
The Justice system broken without a spare.
Where it was once only blind,
now it's deaf and dumb to the truth.

I have seen the working poor get poorer,
blamed for their lack of time and life.
Their wretched broken backs crookedly bent
from the loss they've had to live their whole lives.
And those who have more than they would ever
    need,
cast aspersions in fear of becoming wretched.

I have seen humility replaced by oversized egos,
charity shoved aside for avarice,
with vice gaining speed over virtue,
our moral degradation the welcomed new norm.
Justice has become imprisoned with lost senses,
It's the birth of a new dawn.

Hate is preached in the streets,
from the highways of the worldwide web
to the Houses of Parliaments, Congress
The Pulpits, Tabernacles and Mosques.
They say 'this is all part of the dream,'
I hope we wake up soon enough.

Adrift

Sometimes I don't know where to turn
I turn inside and walk the roads in me
sometimes those roads run dark and deep
occasionally a little light shines within

Sometimes I've retreated so far into me
that I am lost and struggle to stay adrift
you've known how it is to get so lost
quick, toss me an anchor and help me to the shore.

I Got Lost

somewhere along these lines
i got lost

between steamy pots of Jollof rice,
pounded yam and soup
i drowned

along the roads of school runs, recitals,
snotty noses and homework's
i went missing

entwined in naked bedsheets
and bronze thighs
i suffocated

caught in the strictures of expectations
keeping it together and society
i was forgotten

somewhere along these lines
i lost myself

My Child

My child
these were not the dreams
that I had for you;
not for your days to be marked
with running, hiding and cowering
in fear of death that calls before your time.

My child
these were not the dreams
that I had for you;
that your glorious sunset
be blackened by wings of drones and bombing
    planes, ashes, shrapnel's, bloodied and charred
    bodies.

My child
these were not the dreams
that I had for you;
that your sighs are not of pleasure
from the delights of creamy treasure
found in the simple cone of ice and a slice of pie.

My child
these were not the dreams
that I had for you;
that books and the fantastic world
to be found between revered leaves
remain hidden and unknown to you.

My child
these were not the dreams
that I had for you;
that hunger pangs would eat into your guts
driving your eyes deep into their sockets
filled with anguish, want and despair.

My child
these were not the dreams
that I had for you;
that your rich heritage and homeland
bleeds itself to death turning into a field of restless
    souls.

My child
these were the dreams
that I had for you;
simple they may be, I wish
that you look up to see the sun and stars with a
    smile
and at the verdant green of open fields

My child
these were the dreams
that I had for you;
that you dance free, your laughter rich in pleasure
and the mischief of childhood
as you skip through the fountain of life.

My child
these were the dreams
that I had for you;
that your cheeks be cherub
in contentment and joy
your tummy rounded in satisfaction.

My child
these were the dreams
that I had for you;
that your days will be long and well-lived,
filled with bittersweet memories of life.

It's Complicated

Hopping from a bust relationship to the next
in a haste to get over the last,
dragging rattling carcass of soured past along
alas, trailing baggage of past lovers taunt new
    lovers' haven;
infernal struggles, squabbles and the messy details
    repeat
every new day new things uncovered,
a rehash of the past like an old drama playing the
    same lines,
over and over till you get worn out
indeed, this is complicated.

The 'I love you' has long grown cold
slowly burning to indifference,
let us stay together for the children's sake
becomes the mode of agreement
The children are grown and they've flown
now you don't know what to do,
grinding your teeth and staring at the four walls ,
should you go or should you stay goes around in a
    circle;
your world of indifference is safe and comfortable,
indeed, it's so complicated.

You and I belong together
but we can't seem to make it work,
sometimes you make me aggravated,
at other times, I am just fascinated.
I hate you then I love you fiercely,

I want to stomp all over you in madness and rush
    to kiss you better,
a cycle that whirls around, I like the kissing part
    best,
let's stick to the simple things and enjoy being us;
maybe it's not that complicated after all.

Flourish

Let me sit on this branch
evergreen with rich hues of teaching,
where planted droplets of words
cascade over me like jewels,
caught in glistening petals
my flawless carats flourish
under the gaze of the magnified eyes.

Let me sing you a new song
and sprinkle you with pixie dust,
that you may be free to
lose those shackles that hold you bound
and find your way home
so,we run bare feet with no care
in the grassy world of words.

Confined beauty

Didn't mama coo to you
about how gorgeous you are,
even when you were still a nutshell
nestled safely in her womb?

She cradled you to her bosom
rocked and sang you lullabies,
your eyes wide in love
you soaked in all her words.

You must remember her words,
you're beautiful just the way you are,
don't confine your beauty to definitions of anyone
just know that it's true.

Unbridled

Wild and unfettered ruminations
my mind runs along as would a mountain goat,
hopping in a skittish manner
stopping to stare at rainbows, briefly,
it bleats and skips along.

Unharnessed like the mischievous bush monkey
that swings from branch to branch,
resting for a mere moment to snatch a morsel of
    choice,
a pertinent thought paused in mid-swing,
to scratch the surface, to sniff and swing along.

Sashaying down nooks, crannies,
crevices, alleys and hidden aisles,
a young inquisitive miss
searching for a Summer dalliance meets
a hard-lived woman who knows many secrets.

This home to billions of thoughts,
unharnessed, unbridled, wild and free,
tamed, contained, measured and stable,
salacious, pious, decadent and decent,
each a microcosm in microseconds.

They wander through the constant ticking of time,
from known past to present and imaginary future.
This my mind of mine,
an abode of a thousand emotions and thoughts,
quietly brought to peace in the calm of my heart.

All of You

You can't pour all of you
into a heart that creates no room
even for themselves
be bold, be large, be you,
go to places where you are unchained
for you can't squeeze a raging Ocean
like yourself
into a mere Lagoon.

I Know

I don't need you to tell me my strength
I know it
I just need you to be there when I'm soft
I need it
I don't need you to tell me who to become
I know it
I just need you there to watch me become
I want it
I don't need you to make me complete
I know it
I just want you to share out of my wholeness
You need it

The Joy of Pain

My heart I buried in a bottle filled with ice
hid it under layers of calcified debris
in a bid to get away from it all
but pain never failed to come for a call

To poke at parts that hadn't seen the light
with resilience and a hammer,
it hit my head with handheld memories,
plowed into my guts with fists of quivering
    thoughts.

I begged for mercy, but it wouldn't let up.
It shook me up till my shoulders heaved in sobs,
tears streamed down in hot rivulets,
pain reminded me of the sweetness of pleasure.

Unsure, I dug through the grime for the bottle
and brought it out into the light of day.
The glass around my icy heart shattered,
tears from my eyes melted my dismay.

Naptime Dreams

I dreamt at naptime, it was not much of a dream, a
    story or a poem.
A little bird lost the plumes of its tail,
playing a tambourine, it looked beautiful, its naked
    butt stood out
crude and unabashed in the afternoon sun.

I was playing the guitar, I don't play the guitar;
the authentic twang that comes forth from it
    impressed me.
It's not much of a dream, a story or a poem
but its flow pleased me

The naked bird laid a big spotted egg
that hatched six naked beautiful chicklets,
they all danced around in a little circle with their
    tambourines
chirping in rhythm to my guitars twang.

I woke and pondered at the naptime dream
that was not much of a dream, a story or a poem,
I spied a pigeon perched on my window sill,
sadly, its feathers were all intact and it had no
    tambourine.

Morningside

The morning sun amuses itself
caressing the surface of the water
the bluish grey water ripples and glitters
like a gem of immeasurable carats
under the fingers of its beautiful rays

The man in a silhouette and his silver pail
leans on the metal bridge,
his cigarette dangling from the left side of his lips,
his right hand holding the fishing rod,
waiting for a bite to tug the end of the hook

The seagull dives in with perfect precision
coming up with a startled, squiggly fish
whose scales glint in the bright early sun,
and I wonder if it says its last prayer
as the gull gobbles it up

The empty plastic bottle bobbed along
following the flow with intent
as though it had a message to bear
it headed to the shores
where it would end up with piles of other junk

She jogged past in a graceful trot,
hair bounced up and down to her rhythm and
    music,
Fido ran along with his tongue hanging out
pausing often to observe a crab scurrying along
and to leave his pee trail on the beach rock

Man, gull, fish, bottle, girl and dog,
a palette of movement and colours
caught in my eyes' and trapped in my mind
as I witness a casual dance of life
early this day of morning side.

Woven

We gather these memories
over many, many centuries,
intricately woven like filigree laces
they become intrigues of time and places.

When we grow ancient and thigh gaps lost to
    calories,
we sit in rocking chairs lost in reverie,
tossing secrets in the orange flames of the
    fireplace,
fanning the embers of dirty conspiracies.

Sugarcane Baby

Remember the days you and I were mere saplings,
we dreamt sweet dreams like young tenderlings,
woven in Summers afternoon with coloured
     strings
and tied up in boxes decorated with ribbons

Our baths taken in basins, we ate sweet cheap
     candy
and danced to the rhythm of sugar cane baby,
life was certainly rosy and dandy,
vexations easily solved with treats from the pantry

Remember the days you and I were young misses
we dreamt sweet dreams of young lasses,
of fairy-tale princes and tycoons of Mills and Boons
galloping on white steeds and making us swoon

Hair delicately woven in flirty curls,
we shimmied to the dance steps of the current
     twirl,
life was sweet as beautiful pubescent, young girls
waiting for their dreams to unfurl

These days you and I are not Spring chickens,
we've lived a bit, sometimes we feel as old as
     Dickens,
but the thing with dreams is that the plot thickens
if you believe and your heart's still ticking.

Hot flashes, aching joints, forgetfulness and all,
thinning hair, greyness, flatulence and dry vaginas,
rubenesque, we've learnt to laugh at it all
comfortable in wiser skin we share monologue
    tales of the vagina.

Ancient

I went to this place, a new place it was
yet memories of me floated everywhere
as if I was always there.
it felt like home in my spirit,

the sand beneath my feet scrunched in welcome
the ocean's breeze sighed that they had missed me
I went to this place, a new place it was
yet it felt anciently familiar, it knew me too well.

Unforgettable

Wherever I go babe,
wherever the stream of life may carry me,
buried deep, you permeate every cell inside me
you are with me every step of the way

Wherever life's journey takes me,
wherever you may be right now,
baby, you are never far away
for you are ever emblazoned on my mind.

You and I

My forever friend, you and I are entwined;
our meeting is not by happenstance.
We have journeyed through eternity,
our souls, old friends for more than years can
 count.

And though my hand slips out of yours in death
know that I do not die,
for death is not the end,
but just the beginning of you and I.

Inseparable

You and I
are like yesterday
and tomorrow
we are inseparable,

even when the Sun
goes down under
the blanket of the night
our Moon holds us together

Bit by Bit

In little drops,
your love penetrates
it wears down my inhibitions
it breaks down my suspicions.

In steady flow,
your loving motions
grant me buoyancy
taking me to places I never knew.

In rocking rhythm,
I learn how to love
floating beside you
together, we make a beautiful song.

Blended

Him

From the turntable inherited from his old man
crooned smooth, smoky rich tunes of old jazz,
a handful of onions, he tossed into the pan
deftly stirred in the sauce from the bottle,
pleasant, earthy aroma tickled the senses
he cooked like a man in love

Love didn't come in neat packages he thought,
but as a fireball of a woman
whose dark origins drew him in like a spell
wide gleaming eyes flashing in challenge
full lips made him imagine sin
in ways he had never done before.

Her

She hummed to Erykah Badu driving to his street,
a quick glance in the compact mirror
to touch-up powder and gloss, a pat to bold afro
    hair and a dap of the oil musk ,
in delicious anticipation with sweet thoughts
    tucked inside her belly like warm syrup
she hurried up like a woman in love

She didn't know what to do with the love she had
    for him,
falling for him had never been in the books,
sometimes she felt she was his secret pleasure,

taken in between slow nibbles and quick bites
like caramel candy hidden in the dark side of the
    pantry
to be stolen and savoured away from greedy eyes'.

We

We shut-out everyone who said we were not
    meant to be
whose ideologues struggled at the idea of us.
They said, *'lecturer and student,'* that's not quite
    right,
black and white, they simply don't match.
They said we could not straddle both worlds
we had to choose and we chose us.

They believed that we would never last
that our contrasts were too stark
yet our hearts knew the truth
for our love knew no bounds.
What we felt was beyond the skin
our differences made us make it last.

Conjoined

I desire to climb into your soul,
to build a house in there;
where I will lie cradled in your essence
your heartbeat a rhyme to my music.

I hunger to fuse my spirit to yours,
where every fragment of your life's force
conjoins to mine with intensity
till there's no longer you or I.

Love Paintings

Turn my body into a canvas of love paintings,
trace my mind with tendrils of affection,
let my heart be a manuscript of orgasmic love
    notes
that sings an orchestra of our communion.

Though my lips hum sappy love notes,
my eyes starry in bright lights,
my soul knows its compass to home,
that's who you are.

To The Moon and back

Would I go to the moon for you?
Don't count on that my dear man, since I am not an
    astronaut!
Would I want you to go to the moon for me?
If you fancy a jaunt at zero gravity, you are certainly
    most welcome.
I promise to love you till we are both long in the
    tooth,
I promise to love you even when you snore and
    keep me awake,
I promise to love you when you hog the blanket
    and my butt is out in the cold,
I promise to love you and laugh at re-runs of your
    dry jokes,
I promise to love you, wrinkles, warts and all,
But don't get any ideas about doing anything
    foolish,
since I have no plans to go to jail for you.
But, I will be right here,
keeping the kettle warm,
until you return from the Moon.

Night winds of the Gulf

With tops down, your convertible purred along
the night wind flowed in breezy trails
plastering my summer dress, a slip of woven fruits
to rounded curves that loved its gentle caress.

Your arm casually stroked loose tendrils
at the nape of my neck
and in the balmy dark Persian night
it certainly felt just right.

'I love you forever'
I whispered close to your ears
your dreamy reply of *'forever'*
all the answer that I required.

The smell of gasoline from factories
mingled with the queen of the night
your lips shone from Vaseline
wearing a secret smile, they looked inviting.

Inky dark Gulf glimmered under the stars
streetlights beamed along the route of E611
like single fireflies, they twinkled and followed us
as we curved up the hill top to Jebel Hafeet.

The city falls behind with each mile
the music and our laughter interrupted the night
adventures of you and I in dark Summer nights
would keep this heart dreamy for many Winters.

Perfect Union

Her creaky bones made her cranky
his flatulence made him full of fart
her nagging drove him nuts
his mumbling lips made her shout
'what did you say Fred?'

They love each other very much,
they are each other's crutch.
old age came, nothing remained the same,
he was too blind to see the sprouted hairs on her
    chin,
she was too deaf to hear the noisy gas escape his
    chambers,

theirs is still the perfect union.

'

Priceless

I set off to find some treasure
instead, I found much more.

Into the wishing well
I tossed my shiny little coin,

Along you came and handed me a seashell
you gave me the whole ocean,

You made me painted beads
you colourfully decorated my life,

You cut me handwritten cards
you wrote for me a whole new world,

You wrote beautiful poems for me
I saw heaven through your eyes,

I set off to find some treasure
and found priceless, precious you.

Hard Road

I am not worried
about how tight
my shoes pinch
my toes

I could easily
remove them
and walk on
barefoot

I am concerned
about the blisters
growing under
my feet

I could see
the long hard road
stretched ahead of me

Rebirth

A broken heart heals
and a healed heart loves
even deeper than before

Many lives I've lived
some died naturally
some buried unnaturally

These bits and pieces
all tied together
is a rebirth of me

No one, but you
took my tattered pieces
and made a beautiful whole.

Crossroads

Approaching the Autumn of her life
at crossroads with decisions is a strife
afraid to stand still,
too cautious to run forward,
sitting down is not a choice,
but to crawl forward on bent knees, she must
for her to grow and thrive.

On My Way

I walk the fringes of tomorrow
with the dust of yesterday
gathered under my feet

I stare through windows
with longing in my eyes
my desire hanging on my sleeves

I tiptoe forward
with uncertainty tripping me up
not knowing where I'm going but I'm on my way.

The Pen and My Words

With my pen
my words pierced
hearts

With my pen
my words blotted
borders

With my pen
my words drew
blood

With my pen
my words unlocked
tears

With my pen
my words wove
dreams

With my pen
my words instilled
inspiration

With my pen
my words defeated
doubt

With my pen
my words silenced
fear

With my pen
my words changed
impossibilities

With my pen
my words transformed
me

My heart

My heart is no longer a fallow land,
but a peaceful harbour
where you may berth and find rest.

A place to seek sincerity,
a warm open bay, fertile and promising
leading to the island of me,
where exciting chaos melds with tranquillity.

2 am

It's 2 am.
Maybe it's the cold of the air-conditioned room
    that wakes me up,
Maybe it's the bird of thoughts that fly around in
    my head even when my mouth has long ceased
    to talk,
Maybe it's the gritty feel of microscopic desert
    sand, embedded and irritating my skin,
Reminding me that I fell asleep yet again lost in the
    pages of a book, never having taken that shower
    I said that I would take, after the walk.

The house is silent. Hubby is on a trip, the children
    are deeply asleep in their wonderful world of
    snooze,
The clock tick-tocks, in the quiet, it's relentless soft
    sound, sounds loud enough.

The hum of the outside seeps in, I hear the whirr of
    the lift, I hear the drone of cars,
Somewhere there's a cabbie scooting around with
    customers, there are planes bringing in and
    taking away visitors and then there's me.

Wondering if a cup of soup is out of place at this
    hour – opening the fridge to cut a piece of cold
    chicken, along with not taking that shower, I
    forgot to eat and the hunger pangs remind me,

Brief thoughts settle for a walk in my head, I am at
   peace even when pieces of me are torn.
At this wee hour of the night and morning, I feel
   your presence
First, you rest on my head like a Dove, your weight
   is so light but your presence is solid
Then you shift to my right shoulder f––or the
   slightest moment
Then you dive into my heart and nestle inside.

I may not be able to find a temple to lay myself
   down in worship, I may not afford a ticket to
   Rome,
But I feel you because you are here, you didn't
   need a temple to visit me.
I feel you so much that I am suffused with a
   gratitude that I can't describe,

I cease to question sublime moments like your
   presence but to soak in them;
Moments when nothing is perfect,
When all seems as it should be even when
   everything is chaotic and imbalanced.

It's 2.45 am

Always

Countless times she forgot
he reminded her
that his love
is free.

Countless times she doubted
but his steadfastness
was forever
enduring.

Countless times she fell
his right hand
propped her
upright.

Countless troubles called
always, he remained
a tower of
refuge.

When I return

When I am done here, I will go
and I will return as everything;

The Earth and it's beautiful, rugged terrain,
majestic mountains, and the quiet hills
valleys, plateaus, forests and the vast desert

I shall be the wind that you feel, but can't touch
I shall be the gentle and the torrential rain,

I will be the air, the billowing clouds that float by
the waters of all corners of the earth
even the puddle that you step in,

I will be the eagle that soars the skies,
the dove that coos and the watching owl,

I shall be the whale and the dolphin
the plankton, the seaweed
and the beautiful pearl in the oyster's shell,

I will be the dewdrops gathered on the verdant
    green and the pretty, vivid flower blooms

The swift cheetah and the gentle lamb
a kitten and a dog and the rabbit running from the
    fox and yes, I shall be the fox,

The pretty blushing maid in her red shoes,
glossy lips and corn rows
casting flirty looks under thick lashes,

The handsome dark stranger with mysterious eyes
and the cleft in his chin,

The vivacious lady with the laughing eyes
with a loud throaty chuckle and her big black
    purse,

The friendly, robust neighbour down the corner
who always offers cakes and pies,

The mother with a baby suckling at the breast
the suckling child at the mother's breast
each gurgling in joy at the other

The pebble stones and the grain of sand under
    your feet
The music that rouses you to dance and stirs your
    soul

You will see me in the stars, in the skies and in the
    face of everything,
'cos when I am done here, I will go and
I shall return as everything.

Also by Jacqueline Oby-Ikocha

Oby-Ikocha, Jacqueline., (2016). Out of the Silent Breath.

EPUB edition. Moyhill Publishing.
ISBN:9781905597697.
Kindle Edition. Amazon Media EU S.à r.l.2016
ASIN: B01EYN38ES

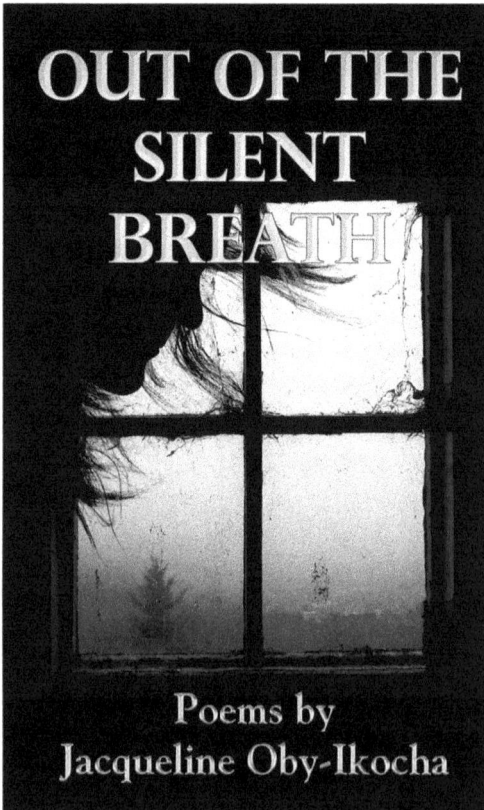

www.ingramcontent.com/pod-product-compliance
Lightning Source LLC
Chambersburg PA
CBHW060030050426
42448CB00012B/2942